Walking in Wisdom: 31 Declarations That Change Everything

By Risa Stegall

Published by Shepherd's Word Publishing

ISBN: 979-8-9988435-3-2

shepherdsword@shepherdswordpublishing.com

31-Day Declaration Booklet

Companion to: The Choice That Changed Everything: Walking in Wisdom in a World of Folly*

Dedication

To everyone seeking to walk in the wisdom of God: May your life be transformed as you declare His truth daily. To my family, friends, and community, thank you for your encouragement. And to the Father,

Son, and Holy Spirit—thank You for Your wisdom, presence, and unfailing guidance.

Table of Contents

Introduction

This booklet is designed to help you walk in wisdom by declaring God's Word daily. Each declaration is rooted in Scripture and aligned with the truth of God's wisdom. As a companion to *The Choice That Changed Everything: Walking in Wisdom in a World of Folly*, this

31day journey invites you to speak life, truth, and victory into every

area of your life through the power of the Father, Son, and Holy Spirit. May the wisdom of God guide you as you declare His promises over your life.

How to Use This Booklet

Each day includes a Scripture, a declaration, and a reflection question. Begin by reading the Scripture aloud, then speak the declaration boldly in faith. Reflect in writing after each day to allow God's wisdom to

deepen in your heart. At the end of the book, you'll find additional

journaling prompts and a closing prayer. Let this journey mark a new season of clarity, discernment, and wisdom.

31-Day Scripture-Based Declarations & Reflections Day 1: Proverbs 4:7 (NKJV)

Scripture:

"Wisdom is the principal thing; therefore get wisdom: and with all thy getting get understanding." — Proverbs 4:7

Declaration:

Today, I choose the wisdom of God. I pursue the wisdom that flows from the Father, revealed through Jesus Christ and guided by the Holy Spirit. I will not lean on my own understanding but will walk in divine counsel. In Jesus' name, Amen.

Biblical Context and Explanation:

The book of Proverbs is a collection of wise sayings, primarily written by King Solomon. Proverbs 4:7 emphasizes the supreme importance of wisdom in the life of a believer. In this passage, Solomon asserts that wisdom is the "principal thing," meaning it is the foundation upon

which everything else in life is built. Wisdom in Scripture is not merely intellectual knowledge but a divine insight that helps guide moral decisions, relationships, and actions according to God's will.

By prioritizing wisdom, we acknowledge that human understanding is limited, and God's wisdom offers clarity and direction that cannot be achieved through worldly methods. Wisdom is both a gift and a pursuit must be actively sought after and cherished.

Character Study – Solomon: The Model of Wisdom

Solomon, known for his unparalleled wisdom, was a man chosen by God to lead Israel. In 1 Kings 3:5-14, God offered Solomon anything he wanted, and Solomon chose wisdom to govern God's people.

Because of his request, God not only gave him wisdom but also wealth and honor, proving that wisdom has both spiritual and practical benefits. Solomon's life exemplified the power of divine wisdom—he made decisions that brought peace, prosperity, and justice to his kingdom, but also wrote down the lessons he learned, providing us with the wisdom found in Proverbs.

Real-Life Example:

Reflecting on Solomon's request for wisdom, how can we apply this model in our own lives? When faced with challenges, we are called to ask for God's wisdom rather than relying on our own limited understanding. Just as Solomon's wisdom was a gift from God, so too is the wisdom available to us. By seeking God's wisdom, we gain not just intellectual knowledge but practical guidance for our daily lives.

Extended Reflection Prompts:

- *How has the wisdom of God influenced the choices you've made in the past?*
- *Can you identify a specific situation where trusting God's wisdom led you to success or peace?*
- *What does "leaning on your own understanding" look like in your life? How do you catch yourself when you're relying too heavily on your own wisdom?*
- *How can you remind yourself to seek God's wisdom today?*

Practical Application/Action Step:

Today, choose one decision to make with wisdom. Pause, pray, and seek God's guidance through Scripture and the Holy Spirit before making it. Keep a journal of your thoughts and insights during this process. Commit to walking in wisdom, trusting that God's direction will lead you down the path of righteousness.

Prayer:

Heavenly Father, I thank You for the wisdom You have so generously given me. I choose to trust Your understanding above my own, and I ask that You guide my thoughts and decisions today. May I rely on the

Holy Spirit for divine counsel, and may Your wisdom be my shield and guide. In Jesus' name, Amen.

Meditative Thought:

"I am choosing wisdom today. The Lord is my guide, and He is leading me to a path of understanding, peace, and growth."

Wisdom Quote:

"The beginning of wisdom is the fear of the Lord. He who does not fear the Lord cannot truly be wise." – C.S. Lewis

5Day 2: James 1:5 (NKJV)

Scripture:

"If any of you lacks wisdom, let him ask of God, who gives to all liberally and without reproach, and it will be given to him." — James 1:5

Declaration:

I ask my Heavenly Father for wisdom, and I receive it through faith in Jesus Christ. The Holy Spirit leads me in truth and clarity. I will not walk in confusion. In Jesus' name, Amen.

Biblical Context and Explanation:

James, the brother of Jesus, wrote this epistle to encourage believers to live out their faith with practical wisdom. In James 1:5, he assures us that God is generous in granting wisdom to those who ask. Unlike worldly wisdom that is limited and self-centered, God's wisdom is pure, untainted by selfish motives. The key to receiving this wisdom is asking in faith, trusting that God will give it abundantly and without hesitation.

This promise reminds us that we are never left to figure things out on our own. When we lack wisdom, we can boldly ask God, knowing that He desires to equip us for every situation.

Character Study – Solomon's Prayer for Wisdom

As mentioned earlier, Solomon's prayer for wisdom (1 Kings 3:5-14) serves as a powerful example. Solomon asked God for wisdom not for selfish gain, but to serve the people he was called to lead. His request pleased God, and in response, God granted him unparalleled wisdom. Similarly, we are encouraged to ask God for wisdom in our own lives, trusting that He will provide exactly what we need for our circumstances.

Real-Life Example:

When you face challenges, do you remember to ask for God's wisdom first? Solomon's story shows us the power of humility in asking God for what we need, not for selfish gain but for the ability to serve others.

Extended Reflection Prompts:

- *In what areas of your life do you feel you need more wisdom?*
- *Do you feel confident in asking God for wisdom? What has held you back in the past from asking?*
- *How can you actively receive God's wisdom in your day-to-day life?*

Practical Application/Action Step:

Take a moment today to ask God for wisdom in a specific area of your life. Write down what you're seeking wisdom for and trust that God will guide you. Make this a daily practice of seeking God's direction in your decisions.

Prayer:

Father, I thank You for the wisdom that You offer freely to all who ask. I believe that You will give me wisdom in every area of my life as I seek You. I ask today for clarity in my decisions and for the strength to walk according to Your will. In Jesus' name, Amen.

Meditative Thought:

"I ask for wisdom, and I trust that God will guide me with clarity and understanding."

Wisdom Quote:

"The wisdom from above is first pure, then peaceable, gentle, open to reason, full of mercy and good fruits, impartial and sincere." – James 3:17

Day 3: Proverbs 3:5–6 (NKJV)

Scripture:
"Trust in the Lord with all your heart, and lean not on your own understanding; in all your ways acknowledge Him, and He shall direct your paths." — Proverbs 3:5–6

Declaration:

I trust in the Lord with all my heart. I surrender my understanding to the wisdom of the Trinity. I acknowledge the Father, Son, and Holy Spirit in all I do, and my path is made straight. In Jesus' name, Amen.

Biblical Context and Explanation:

These verses are some of the most well-known and cherished in Proverbs. King Solomon, the author of Proverbs, speaks from a place of experience, urging us to trust God fully and not rely on our limited understanding. Trusting God means acknowledging Him in every aspect of our lives, and doing so leads to clear direction. When we put our trust in Him, He promises to guide our paths and make them straight. This verse invites us to choose faith over fear, to surrender our thoughts and plans to God, knowing that His guidance will always be better than our own.

Character Study – Abraham's Trust in God

Abraham's journey is a prime example of trusting God's direction. In Genesis 12:1, God told Abraham to leave his homeland and go to a land He would show him. Abraham trusted God without knowing the

full picture, and through his faith, God led him to greatness. Abraham's life is a testimony to trusting in God's plan even when the path is unclear.

Real-Life Example:

Think of a time when you trusted God's guidance, even though it was difficult or uncertain. How did trusting Him shape the outcome? Was it worth it in the end?

Extended Reflection Prompts:

- *When you feel confused or uncertain, how do you respond? Do you lean on your own understanding or seek God's guidance first?*
- *Reflect on a time when you trusted God's guidance despite not understanding the full picture. What was the result?*
- *What can you do today to acknowledge God in all your ways?*

Practical Application/Action Step:

Today, choose one area where you feel uncertain and consciously surrender your understanding to God. Acknowledge Him in that decision and ask for His direction. Journal what you feel prompted to do and how God responds.

Prayer:

Lord, I trust You with all my heart. I choose to lean not on my own understanding but to trust in Your perfect wisdom. Guide my steps today and direct my paths according to Your will. In Jesus' name, Amen.

Meditative Thought:

"I trust in the Lord with all my heart, knowing He will lead me where I need to go."

Wisdom Quote:

"Trusting God will never lead you down the wrong path." – *Anonymous*

Day 4: Psalm 111:10 (NKJV)

Scripture:

"The fear of the Lord is the beginning of wisdom; a good

understanding have all those who do His commandments. His praise endures forever." — Psalm 111:10

Declaration:
I walk in holy reverence before the Lord. The fear of God is the foundation of wisdom in my life. I delight in obeying His Word through the strength of the Holy Spirit. In Jesus' name, Amen.

Biblical Context and Explanation:

Psalm 111 is a hymn of praise that declares the greatness of God's works.

Verse 10 highlights that the fear of the Lord is the beginning of wisdom. "Fear" here refers to a deep respect and reverence for God, not a fear of punishment. It is acknowledging God's sovereignty, holiness, and goodness. True wisdom begins with this foundational respect, and it guides our lives toward righteous living.

This verse reminds us that living in reverence to God and obeying His commandments is the path to wisdom.

Character Study – Daniel's Reverence for God

Daniel exemplifies the "fear of the Lord" in his life. Despite being in a foreign land and facing pressure to compromise his faith, Daniel chose to honor God with his actions (Daniel 1:8). His reverence for God and commitment to following His commandments led to wisdom and favor, even in the midst of difficult circumstances.

Real-Life Example:

Reflect on how living with reverence for God has impacted your choices. Have you ever made a difficult decision because of your respect for God's ways?

Extended Reflection Prompts:

*   *How do you show reverence for God in your daily life?*
    *   *What role does the 'fear of the Lord' play in the way you make decisions?*
    *   *How can reverence for God shape the way you view challenges or temptations in your life?*

Practical Application/Action Step:

Today, find one opportunity to show reverence for God in your actions—whether in your work, interactions, or personal time. Make a choice that reflects your honor for His commands.

Prayer:

Heavenly Father, I honor You and revere Your holiness. I choose to live in awe of Your greatness and to follow Your ways. May my decisions

today reflect my reverence for You and bring glory to Your name. In Jesus' name, Amen.

Meditative Thought:

"The beginning of wisdom is honoring God in all that I do."

Wisdom Quote:

"The fear of the Lord is the beginning of wisdom; all who follow His precepts have good understanding." – Psalm 111:10

Day 5: Ecclesiastes 7:12 (NKJV)

Scripture:

"For wisdom is a defense as money is a defense, but the excellence of knowledge is that wisdom gives life to those who have it." —

Ecclesiastes 7:12

Declaration:

God's wisdom is my shield and my source of life. The knowledge of the Father, secured through Jesus Christ, and revealed by the Holy Spirit preserves and empowers me. In Jesus' name, Amen.

Biblical Context and Explanation:

In Ecclesiastes, Solomon, the author, reflects on the meaning of life and the value of wisdom. In this verse, he compares wisdom to a

defense, much like money, but highlights that wisdom offers a more

valuable defense: the protection and life it provides. Wisdom does not only protect us from physical dangers but also from the challenges of life that can harm our spirit. It empowers us to live in alignment with God's will.

Character Study – Joseph's Wisdom in Adversity

Joseph's wisdom was tested in many ways. He was betrayed by his brothers, sold into slavery, and falsely accused, yet through all of it, God gave him wisdom to navigate each challenge.

Joseph's life shows how wisdom can protect and sustain us in the face of hardship (Genesis 41).

Real-Life Example:

Think of a time when God's wisdom provided protection or guidance in a difficult or challenging situation. How did wisdom act as a shield for you?

Extended Reflection Prompts:

- *In what ways has God's wisdom protected and strengthened you?*
- *What situations have you encountered where wisdom helped you avoid danger or made a difficult situation easier to handle?*
- *How can you actively apply wisdom in your current challenges?*

Practical Application/Action Step:

Think of a current challenge you are facing. Seek God's wisdom through prayer and reflection, trusting that it will shield and guide you through it.

Prayer:

Lord, thank You for the protection and life that wisdom brings. I ask for Your wisdom to guide me through today's challenges.

May it shield me, strengthen me, and lead me toward the fullness of life You have promised. In Jesus' name, Amen.

Meditative Thought:

"Wisdom is my defense, and in it, I find life and protection."

Wisdom Quote:

"Wisdom is the principal thing; therefore, get wisdom, and with all your getting, get understanding." – Proverbs 4:7

Day 6: Colossians 3:16 (NKJV)

Scripture:

"Let the word of Christ dwell in you richly in all wisdom, teaching and admonishing one another in psalms and hymns and spiritual songs,

singing with grace in your hearts to the Lord."

— Colossians 3:16

Declaration:

The Word of Christ dwells in me richly. The wisdom of God flows through my heart and mind. By the power of the Holy Spirit, I speak, live, and act with grace and understanding. In Jesus' name, Amen.

Biblical Context and Explanation:

In this verse, Paul encourages the Colossians to allow the Word of Christ to live deeply within them. Wisdom is not just an intellectual exercise but an active, transformative force that shapes our actions,

speech, and relationships. The richness of God's Word leads to a life of wisdom, peace, and grace. This scripture reminds us that wisdom is

not only about knowledge but also about how we live it out in our interactions with others.

Character Study – Jesus, the Word Made Flesh

Jesus is the ultimate embodiment of the Word of God. John 1:14 tells us that "the Word became flesh and dwelt among us." His life was the perfect expression of divine wisdom. Every action, teaching, and

decision Jesus made was rooted in the wisdom of God. By following His example, we too can live wisely, letting God's Word dwell in us richly.

Real-Life Example:

Think about how living according to God's Word has shaped your life. Has reading Scripture given you insight or understanding that helped you make wise decisions in difficult times?

Extended Reflection Prompts:

- *How does the Word of Christ dwell in your life today?*
- *What Scriptures have impacted you the most in your walk with God?*
- *How can you allow God's Word to guide your thoughts, words, and actions more deeply?*

Practical Application/Action Step:

Take time today to read a passage of Scripture and reflect on how it can influence your actions and decisions. Consider sharing a verse with someone who may need encouragement today.

Prayer:

Lord, let Your Word dwell richly within me. May Your wisdom guide my heart, mind, and actions. Help me to speak with grace, live with understanding, and reflect Your truth in all that I do. In Jesus' name, Amen.

Meditative Thought:

"The Word of Christ dwells richly in me, shaping my thoughts, words, and life."

Wisdom Quote:

*"The Word of God is a lamp to our feet and a light to our path." –
Psalm 119:105*

Day 7: Proverbs 2:6 (NKJV)

Scripture:
*"For the Lord gives wisdom; from His mouth come knowledge and
understanding."* — Proverbs 2:6

Declaration:

The Lord pours out wisdom into my life. I receive divine

understanding and knowledge through Jesus and by the leading of the
Holy Spirit. I walk in supernatural insight. In Jesus' name, Amen.

Biblical Context and Explanation:

Proverbs 2 focuses on the blessings that come with seeking wisdom.
This verse underscores the fact that wisdom comes directly from God.

It is not merely the accumulation of knowledge, but a divine gift that
leads to understanding and insight. By seeking God's wisdom, we are
aligning ourselves with His perfect plan for our lives.

Character Study – Solomon's Request for Wisdom

Solomon's request for wisdom (1 Kings 3:5-14) is one of the clearest
examples of how wisdom is a gift from God. When Solomon asked for
wisdom, God granted him understanding beyond measure.

Solomon's wisdom was not only intellectual but spiritual, allowing him to lead Israel with righteousness and fairness. Similarly, we too can ask God for wisdom and trust that He will provide us with the insight needed to navigate life.

Real-Life Example:

Think of a time when you asked God for wisdom, and He gave you clarity or understanding. How did this divine wisdom guide your decisions?

Extended Reflection Prompts:

- *In what areas of your life do you need more wisdom?*
- *What does it mean to "walk in supernatural insight"? How can you do this in your daily life?*
- *How can you be more intentional about seeking wisdom from God rather than relying on your own understanding?*

Practical Application/Action Step:

Today, identify one area where you need more wisdom and ask God to provide insight. Spend time in prayer and wait for His guidance, trusting that He will answer generously.

Prayer:

Father, I thank You for the wisdom You generously give.

I open my heart to receive Your understanding today. Help me to walk in divine insight, trusting Your wisdom in every decision. In Jesus' name, Amen.

Meditative Thought:

"God gives wisdom generously, and I choose to receive it today."

Wisdom Quote:

"If any of you lacks wisdom, let him ask of God, who gives to all liberally and without reproach." – James 1:5

Day 8: Matthew 7:24 (NKJV)

Scripture:

"Therefore, whoever hears these sayings of Mine, and does them, I will liken him to a wise man who built his house on the rock." — Matthew 7:24

Declaration:

I build my life on the teachings of Jesus Christ. The rock of my

salvation stands firm, and the Holy Spirit strengthens my foundation with wisdom. In Jesus' name, Amen.

Biblical Context and Explanation:

This verse is part of the Sermon on the Mount, where Jesus teaches the importance of putting His words into practice. He compares those who listen and obey His teachings to a wise builder who builds his house on a rock, which is firm and immovable. Wisdom is not just about knowing God's Word but about applying it in our daily lives. When we live according to Christ's teachings, we build a strong foundation that can withstand life's challenges.

Character Study – The Wise Builder

The wise builder is someone who not only hears but also applies God's Word. This principle is demonstrated throughout Scripture, where wisdom leads to a life built on the solid foundation of Christ. In contrast, the foolish builder who ignores God's Word builds his life on unstable ground, which leads to destruction. Our actions must align with God's truth to create a lasting legacy.

Real-Life Example:

Reflect on a time when applying God's Word provided stability or peace in your life. How did obedience to His teachings serve as a strong foundation in that situation?

Extended Reflection Prompts:

- *What does it look like to build your life on the rock of Jesus' teachings?*

- *How can you ensure that your decisions align with God's Word?*
- *Are there areas in your life where you need to apply God's wisdom more faithfully?*

Practical Application/Action Step:

Take time today to reflect on one area where you need to apply God's Word more intentionally. Make a plan to align your actions with His teachings in that area.

Prayer:

Lord, I choose to build my life on Your Word. Help me to live

according to Your teachings, making Your wisdom the foundation of my decisions. Strengthen my faith and guide my steps today. In Jesus' name, Amen.

Meditative Thought:

"I build my life on the rock of Christ, knowing His Word will never fail."

Wisdom Quote:

"The wise man builds his house upon the rock." – Matthew 7:24

Day 9: Proverbs 13:20 (NKJV) Scripture:

"He who walks with wise men will be wise, but the companion of fools will be destroyed." — Proverbs 13:20

Declaration:

I walk with the wise, guided by the counsel of the Holy Spirit. The Father surrounds me with godly influences that sharpen and refine me in wisdom. In Jesus' name, Amen.

Biblical Context and Explanation:

This verse speaks to the importance of relationships in shaping our

lives. Wisdom is not just about personal understanding; it is also about the company we keep. Proverbs emphasizes the impact that wise

counsel can have, and conversely, how negative influences can lead to destruction. Walking with wise people sharpens our understanding and helps us grow, while walking with fools can derail our progress and

lead to harm.

Character Study – Solomon's Relationship with Wisdom
Solomon, known for his wisdom, often surrounded himself with wise counselors, such as the prophets Nathan and Gad. He understood that wisdom thrives in community and with the right influences.

In contrast, those who isolate themselves or seek out foolish company will lack the guidance needed to live wisely.

Real-Life Example:

Consider the people you associate with regularly. Do they encourage you toward wisdom? How can you surround yourself with individuals who will help you grow in wisdom?

Extended Reflection Prompts:

- *Who are the wise people in your life that God has surrounded you with?*
- *How have they helped shape your wisdom?*
- *What steps can you take to build stronger relationships with wise individuals?*

Practical Application/Action Step:

Identify one person in your life who exemplifies wisdom. Spend time with them today, seeking their counsel and learning from their example.

Prayer:

Father, thank You for surrounding me with wise influences. Help me to walk in wisdom and seek counsel from those who are guided by Your truth. May I be a source of wisdom to others as well. In Jesus' name, Amen.

Meditative Thought:

"I choose to walk with the wise, knowing their counsel leads me toward growth."

Wisdom Quote:

"A wise man is strong, yes, a man of knowledge increases strength." – *Proverbs 24:5*

Day 10: Isaiah 11:2 (NKJV) Scripture:

"The Spirit of the Lord shall rest upon Him, the Spirit of wisdom and

understanding, the Spirit of counsel and might, the Spirit of knowledge and of the fear of the Lord." — Isaiah 11:2

Declaration:

The Holy Spirit, the Spirit of wisdom, rests upon me. I am empowered by God to understand, discern, and walk wisely through every season. In Jesus' name, Amen.

Biblical Context and Explanation:

Isaiah 11:2 prophesies about the Messiah, Jesus Christ, and describes the anointing of the Holy Spirit upon Him. The Spirit of wisdom, understanding, counsel, and knowledge is the same Spirit that empowers believers today. Through the Holy Spirit, we have access to divine wisdom that transcends our natural understanding.

Character Study – Jesus and the Spirit of Wisdom

Jesus lived by the wisdom of the Holy Spirit throughout His ministry. The Spirit empowered Him to heal, teach, and guide people toward the truth. Similarly, the Holy Spirit is given to believers to guide them into all truth and to live wisely.

Real-Life Example:

Reflect on how the Holy Spirit has led you in moments of

decision making. How has He provided wisdom and insight when you needed it most?

Extended Reflection Prompts:

- *How can you cultivate a deeper relationship with the Holy Spirit to grow in wisdom and understanding?*
- *What specific areas of your life would benefit from more of the Spirit's wisdom?*
- *How do you allow the Holy Spirit to guide your thoughts and decisions?*

Practical Application/Action Step:

Spend a few moments today inviting the Holy Spirit to lead you in wisdom. Pray specifically for His guidance in a particular area of your life and trust that He will speak clearly to you.

Prayer:

Holy Spirit, I welcome You to guide me in wisdom and understanding. Empower me to walk wisely through every situation, and help me to rely on Your counsel. In Jesus' name, Amen.

Meditative Thought:

"The Spirit of wisdom rests upon me, guiding my decisions and leading me to truth."

Wisdom Quote:

"The fear of the Lord is the beginning of wisdom, and knowledge of the Holy One is understanding." – Proverbs 9:10

Day 11: Proverbs 1:7 (NKJV)

Scripture:

"The fear of the Lord is the beginning of knowledge, but fools despise wisdom and instruction." — Proverbs 1:7

Declaration:

I honor the Lord and receive His instruction. Knowledge is mine through Jesus, and I embrace wisdom as a gift of the Spirit. In Jesus' name, Amen.

Biblical Context and Explanation:

In Proverbs, Solomon lays the foundation for wisdom by emphasizing the importance of reverence for God. This verse highlights that true knowledge and wisdom begin with the fear of the Lord—respecting and honoring His sovereignty and commands. Without this foundational respect, wisdom is elusive, but with it, we gain understanding and direction for all aspects of life.

Character Study – Solomon's Search for Wisdom

Solomon, known for his extraordinary wisdom, understood that reverence for God was the root of all true wisdom. In 1 Kings 3:9-12, when Solomon asked God for wisdom to rule justly, God granted his request, making him the wisest man to ever live. His reverence for God led to a life filled with insight, prosperity, and peace.

Real-Life Example:

How has honoring God in your decisions led to wisdom? Reflect on a time when you made a choice that demonstrated reverence for God and how that influenced the outcome.

Extended Reflection Prompts:

- *How does honoring God impact your pursuit of wisdom?*
- *In what ways can you express a deeper reverence for Him in your daily life?*
- *What area of your life would be transformed if you honored God more deeply?*

Practical Application/Action Step:

Take time today to express reverence for God in your actions. Whether through prayer, service, or obedience, make a conscious decision to honor Him in your choices today.

Prayer:

Father, I honor You and seek Your wisdom. Help me to value Your

instruction above all else and to live in reverence for You. Guide me in all my decisions today, and may Your wisdom lead me toward peace and understanding. In Jesus' name, Amen.

Meditative Thought:

"Reverence for God is the foundation of wisdom, and I choose to honor Him in all things."

Wisdom Quote:

"The fear of the Lord is the beginning of wisdom, and knowledge of the Holy One is understanding." – Proverbs 9:10

Day 12: 1 Corinthians 1:30 (NKJV)

Scripture:

"But of Him you are in Christ Jesus, who became for us wisdom from God—and righteousness and sanctification and redemption." — 1 Corinthians 1:30

Declaration:

Jesus Christ is my wisdom. I am rooted in Him and guided by His Spirit. The wisdom of God lives in me and leads my every step. In Jesus' name, Amen.

Biblical Context and Explanation:

In 1 Corinthians 1:30, Paul reminds believers that Christ is not just our Savior but also our wisdom. Through Him, we are granted divine insight and understanding, which empowers us to live according to God's will. Jesus, as the wisdom of God, brings righteousness,

sanctification, and redemption, giving us everything we need to live a godly life.

Character Study – Jesus: The Embodiment of Wisdom

Jesus is the ultimate example of wisdom. In His teachings, actions, and sacrifice, He displayed perfect wisdom. John 14:6 tells us that He is

the way, the truth, and the life—embodying God's wisdom in every

way. As believers, we are called to walk in His wisdom, drawing from His example and teachings.

Real-Life Example:

Think about a situation where you sought Jesus' guidance and how His wisdom provided clarity and direction. Reflect on how His teachings

shape your decisions today.

Extended Reflection Prompts:

- *How can you embody the wisdom of Christ in your daily decisions?*
- *What areas of your life do you need to surrender to Christ's wisdom?*
- *How can you deepen your relationship with Jesus to grow in wisdom?*

Practical Application/Action Step:

Today, take a moment to reflect on one area where you need Jesus' wisdom. Spend time in prayer, asking Him to guide you through His wisdom. Commit to following His example in that situation.

Prayer:

Father, in the name of Jesus, I thank You for being my wisdom. Guide my thoughts, decisions, and actions today, and help me to walk in Your wisdom. May Your Spirit empower me to live according to Your truth and follow Your example in every area of my life. In Jesus name, Amen.

Meditative Thought:

"Christ is my wisdom, and in Him, I find all the understanding I need for life."

Wisdom Quote:

"Wisdom is not a trait you possess; it is a life you live in Christ." – *Anonymous*

Day 13: Proverbs 15:33 (NKJV) Scripture:

"The fear of the Lord is the instruction of wisdom, and before honor is humility."

— Proverbs 15:33

Declaration:

I walk in humility and holy reverence before the Lord. Wisdom

instructs me, and the Holy Spirit positions me for honor. In Jesus' name, Amen.

Biblical Context and Explanation:

This verse emphasizes the relationship between humility, wisdom, and honor. The fear of the Lord (reverence for Him) leads to wisdom, and true wisdom begins with humility. Those who are humble before God receive honor, as they align their lives with His will, rather than

seeking self-exaltation. Wisdom and humility go hand in hand, guiding us toward a life of integrity and honor.

Character Study – Moses: A Humble Leader

Moses, often described as the humblest man on earth (Numbers 12:3), exemplifies this principle. His humility before God allowed him to be used as a powerful instrument for God's purposes. Despite his status as

34

leader of Israel, Moses never sought honor for himself but always sought God's will. His humility positioned him to receive great wisdom, which helped him lead Israel to freedom.

Real-Life Example:

Think about how humility has shaped your ability to receive wisdom. Have you ever experienced a situation where humility opened the door to greater understanding or honor?

Extended Reflection Prompts:

- *How has humility shaped your journey to wisdom?*
- *Are there areas where you need to embrace humility more fully in order to walk in greater wisdom?*
- *How does God's wisdom shape the way you interact with others, especially when it comes to humility and honor?*

Practical Application/Action Step:

Take time today to practice humility by serving others or listening carefully to their counsel. Be open to receiving wisdom from those around you, especially those who may challenge your perspective.

Prayer:

Father, I choose humility today, knowing that true wisdom begins with reverence for You. Help me to walk in humility and to honor You in all things. May Your wisdom guide me and lead me to a life of integrity and honor. In Jesus' name, Amen.

Meditative Thought:

"Humility is the key that unlocks wisdom, and I choose to walk in it today."

Wisdom Quote:

"The humble will receive wisdom, and their lives will be filled with honor." – Anonymous

---

Day 14: James 3:17 (NKJV)

Scripture:

"But the wisdom that is from above is first pure, then peaceable,

gentle, willing to yield, full of mercy and good fruits, without partiality and without hypocrisy." — James 3:17

Declaration:

I receive wisdom from above pure and peaceable. The fruit of the Holy Spirit flows from my life as I yield to His leading. In Jesus' name, Amen.

Biblical Context and Explanation:

James contrasts earthly wisdom, which is self-centered and divisive, with heavenly wisdom, which is marked by purity, peace, gentleness, and mercy. This divine wisdom flows from God's character and is reflected in the life of a believer who submits to the Holy Spirit's guidance. When we yield to God's wisdom, it transforms our relationships and actions, bringing peace and righteousness.

Character Study – The Life of Jesus

Jesus exemplified the wisdom that is pure, peaceable, and merciful. In His interactions, He was gentle with the weak, merciful to the sinner, and uncompromising in truth. His life embodied the wisdom that James describes, and His example shows us how to live with integrity, love, and peace.

Real-Life Example:

Reflect on how you can embody this wisdom in your relationships. Have you recently responded to someone with gentleness or mercy? How did that shape the situation?

Extended Reflection Prompts:

- *How can you practice gentleness, mercy, and good fruit as signs of the wisdom you receive from God?*
- *In what areas of your life do you need to yield more fully to God's wisdom?*
- *How does heavenly wisdom affect the way you interact with others, especially those who may not treat you kindly?*

Practical Application/Action Step:

Today, focus on one relationship where you can practice gentleness and mercy. Respond with a heart of peace, seeking reconciliation or understanding. Reflect on how yielding to God's wisdom leads to better outcomes.

Prayer:

Lord, I ask for wisdom from above—pure, peaceable, and merciful. Help me to reflect Your wisdom in all my relationships. May Your fruit flow through me, bringing peace and healing to those around me. In Jesus' name, Amen.

Meditative Thought:

"Heavenly wisdom brings peace and fruitfulness, and I choose to walk in it today."

Wisdom Quote:

"True wisdom is gentle, yielding, and full of mercy—this is the wisdom from above." – Anonymous

---

Day 15: Proverbs 24:3-4 (NKJV)

Scripture:
"Through wisdom a house is built, and by understanding it is

established; by knowledge the rooms are filled with all precious and pleasant riches." — Proverbs 24:3-4

Declaration:

I build my home on God's wisdom. The Holy Spirit establishes every room with peace, love, and understanding. My life is full through Christ. In Jesus' name, Amen.

Biblical Context and Explanation:

Proverbs 24:3-4 teaches that wisdom is the foundation of a well-ordered life, both personally and within our homes. Godly wisdom provides the structure, understanding adds stability, and knowledge fills our lives with precious treasures—both material and spiritual. A home built on these principles will be filled with peace, love, and prosperity, as it is rooted in God's truth.

Character Study – The Wisdom of the Proverbs Woman

Proverbs 31 describes the ideal woman who builds her household with wisdom. She is wise in her decisions, careful with her time, and considerate of her family's needs. Her wisdom brings prosperity, peace, and honor to her home. This model of wisdom is something that we can all strive to cultivate, whether in our families, workplaces, or personal lives.

Real-Life Example:

Think about how God's wisdom has impacted your relationships or home life. Have you made decisions based on wisdom that brought peace and prosperity to your family?

Extended Reflection Prompts:

- *What does it look like to build your home, family, and relationships on the wisdom of God?*
- *How can you establish your household in peace and understanding through His wisdom?*
- *What steps can you take today to ensure that your life is built on the wisdom and knowledge of God?*

Practical Application/Action Step:

Reflect on your relationships and home life today. How can you apply God's wisdom to strengthen these areas? Whether in communication, decision-making, or providing for your family, seek wisdom in every action.

Prayer:

Lord, I thank You for the wisdom that builds strong homes and

relationships. I invite Your wisdom into every part of my life. Establish my home with peace, love, and understanding, and may it reflect Your glory. In Jesus' name, Amen.

Meditative Thought:

"God's wisdom builds a life of peace and prosperity, and I choose to build mine on His truth."

Wisdom Quote:

"A house built on wisdom will stand firm, and its rooms will be filled with all good things." – Anonymous

---

Day 16: Ephesians 5:15-16 (NKJV) *Scripture:*

'...See then that you walk circumspectly, not as fools but as wise,

redeeming the time, because the days are evil.' — Ephesians 5:15-16

Declaration:

'I walk in wisdom, empowered by the Spirit of God. I redeem the time and live with intention, as led by Jesus Christ for such a time as this. In Jesus' name, Amen.'

Biblical Context and Explanation:

Paul encourages believers to walk wisely, redeeming the time, because the days are evil. Time is a precious resource, and we must use it

wisely in service to God. Walking circumspectly requires wisdom that directs every step toward God's purposes.

Character Study – The Apostle Paul:

Paul exemplified the redeeming of time by spreading the gospel relentlessly. Even in prison, Paul used his time to write letters of encouragement and teaching, maximizing each moment for God's glory.

Real-Life Example:

Reflect on how you've used an opportunity wisely, despite challenges. How did wisdom help you maximize the moment?

Extended Reflection Prompts:

- In what ways are you redeeming your time for God's purposes?
- How do you prioritize wisdom in your daily actions?
- What areas of your life need to be redeemed by God's wisdom?

Practical Application/Action Step:

Identify one decision today where you will consciously redeem your time for God's purpose. Write it down and commit to making that decision wisely.

Prayer:

Father, help me to redeem the time I've been given. I want to use every moment for Your glory. Grant me wisdom to prioritize what matters most and walk according to Your will. In Jesus' name, Amen.

Meditative Thought:

'Every moment is an opportunity to live for God and make wise choices.'

Wisdom Quote:

'Time is a gift from God; how you use it is your gift back to Him.' – Anonymous

---

Day 17: Proverbs 8:11 (NKJV) *Scripture:*

'For wisdom is better than rubies, and all the things one may desire cannot be compared with her.' — Proverbs 8:11

Declaration:

'I treasure God's wisdom above all riches. Nothing I desire compares to the wisdom that comes from the Father, through the Son, and revealed by the Holy Spirit. In Jesus' name, Amen.'

Biblical Context and Explanation:

Wisdom is more valuable than any earthly treasure. It brings understanding, peace, and fulfillment. Proverbs teaches that wisdom's worth exceeds that of the finest jewels, gold, or silver.

Character Study – King Solomon:

Solomon's request for wisdom over wealth exemplifies his understanding of true value. God granted him wisdom and wealth because Solomon valued wisdom above all else (1 Kings 3:11-13).

Real-Life Example:

Reflect on a time when choosing wisdom over wealth brought peace or success. How did it impact your life?

Extended Reflection Prompts:

- How do you prioritize wisdom over material things?
- What worldly desires do you need to surrender in exchange for wisdom?
- How can you cultivate a deeper appreciation for wisdom in your life?

Practical Application/Action Step:

Today, choose to value wisdom over anything material. Reflect on one decision where wisdom will be your greatest treasure.

Prayer:

Father, help me to treasure wisdom above all things. May I choose Your understanding over anything this world offers. Guide me to live according to Your wisdom in every situation. In Jesus' name, Amen.

Meditative Thought:

'I choose wisdom over wealth, for it leads me to a deeper relationship with God.'

Wisdom Quote:

'Wisdom is more precious than jewels, and nothing you desire can compare with it.' – Proverbs 8:11

Day 18: Proverbs 9:10 (NKJV) *Scripture:*

'The fear of the Lord is the beginning of wisdom, and the knowledge of the Holy One is understanding.' — Proverbs 9:10

Declaration:

'I reverence the Lord and grow in the knowledge of the Holy One.

Wisdom begins here, and I embrace the understanding the Spirit reveals. In Jesus' name, Amen.'

Biblical Context and Explanation:

Wisdom begins with the fear of the Lord, meaning we honor and respect His holiness and sovereignty. This reverence opens our hearts to understanding and allows wisdom to shape our decisions.

Character Study – Solomon's Reverence for God:

Solomon's wisdom began with his reverence for God's authority (1 Kings 3:9-12). This foundation led him to ask for wisdom above all else, which brought peace and prosperity to his reign.

Real-Life Example:

Reflect on how honoring God has shaped your decisions. Have you experienced a shift in perspective when you prioritize reverence for God?

Extended Reflection Prompts:

- How does reverence for God impact your daily life?
- What role does the 'fear of the Lord' play in your decisions?
- How can reverence for God shape the way you approach challenges or decisions?

Practical Application/Action Step:

Today, focus on honoring God in one area of your life. Seek His wisdom in that situation and reflect on how this shapes your perspective.

Prayer:
Lord, I honor You and seek Your wisdom. Help me to grow in

reverence for You and apply Your wisdom in all areas of my life. In Jesus' name, Amen.

Meditative Thought:

'The fear of the Lord is the beginning of wisdom, and I choose to live in that reverence today.'

Wisdom Quote:

'Wisdom begins with reverence for God and knowledge of the Holy One.' – Proverbs 9:10

Day 19: Proverbs 10:8 (NKJV) *Scripture:*

'The wise in heart will receive commands, but a prating fool will fall.'

— Proverbs 10:8

Declaration:

'I am wise in heart and open to God's commands. I listen, learn, and walk in spiritual maturity, guided by the Holy Spirit. In Jesus' name, Amen.'

Biblical Context and Explanation:

Wisdom involves receiving and obeying God's commands. The wise follow God's direction, while the foolish disregard it. Obedience leads to spiritual growth and maturity, allowing us to reflect God's truth.

Character Study – Daniel's Wisdom and Obedience:

Daniel exemplified wisdom in his obedience to God's laws, even when facing great adversity. His ability to remain steadfast in his faith and principles resulted in divine favor and wisdom from God (Daniel 1:8).

Real-Life Example:

Reflect on a time when you obeyed God's wisdom and saw positive results. How did it impact your life?

Extended Reflection Prompts:

• How can you be more open to receiving and following God's commands?
• What areas of your life require greater obedience to God's wisdom?
• How can obedience lead to spiritual growth and maturity?

Practical Application/Action Step:

Reflect on one area where you need to obey God more fully. Commit to taking obedient steps in that area today.

Prayer:
Lord, I choose to listen to Your commands and walk in obedience. Open my heart to receive Your wisdom and help me to follow Your leading in every situation. In Jesus' name, Amen.

Meditative Thought:

'Obedience to God's Word leads to wisdom and spiritual maturity.'

Wisdom Quote:

'The wise in heart will receive commands and grow in wisdom.' – Proverbs 10:8

Day 20: Proverbs 20:18 (NKJV) *Scripture:*

"Plans are established by counsel; by wise counsel wage war." — Proverbs 20:18

Declaration:

I seek wise counsel and make Spirit-led decisions. I do not fight in the flesh, but with divine strategy and peace from above. In Jesus' name, Amen.

Biblical Context and Explanation:

Wisdom in decision-making, particularly in times of conflict, is essential. Proverbs teaches that strategic planning and seeking counsel are key to successful outcomes. By listening to wise counsel, we align ourselves with God's direction and avoid foolish mistakes.

Character Study – David's Strategic Counsel:

King David often sought the Lord's counsel through the prophets and priests during his reign. Even in battle, he relied on God's guidance (1 Samuel 23:2). This reliance on God's wisdom helped him lead Israel to victory.

Real-Life Example:

Think of a time when seeking wisdom and counsel led to victory or success. How did the advice of others help you avoid failure?

Extended Reflection Prompts:

- In what areas of your life do you need to seek wise counsel?
- How can seeking God's wisdom and counsel bring peace and victory in your life?
- What steps can you take today to align your plans with God's will?

Practical Application/Action Step:

Ask God today to guide you in seeking wise counsel for a decision you need to make. Take action with faith, trusting that God's wisdom will lead you to victory.

Prayer:

Lord, I seek Your wisdom and counsel. Help me to make Spirit-led decisions and follow Your guidance in all things. In Jesus' name, Amen.

Meditative Thought:

'Wise counsel leads to victory, and I choose to seek it today.'

Wisdom Quote:

'Plans are established by counsel, and by wise counsel, we succeed.' – Proverbs 20:18

Day 21: Proverbs 21:30 (NKJV) *Scripture:*

"There is no wisdom or understanding or counsel against the Lord." — Proverbs 21:30

Declaration:

I trust in the wisdom of God. No plan or counsel can stand against His will. I submit to His guidance, and His wisdom leads me to victory. In Jesus' name, Amen.

Biblical Context and Explanation:

This verse emphasizes the supremacy of God's wisdom over any human understanding or strategy. No matter how much knowledge or counsel we seek, God's wisdom is unmatched and always leads to the best outcome.

Character Study – The Foolishness of Men's Plans:

In the book of Esther, Haman's plans to destroy the Jews were foiled by God's wisdom. Despite all his plotting, God's counsel prevailed, demonstrating that no plan can stand against the will of God (Esther 7:10).

Real-Life Example:

Reflect on a time when your plans didn't work out as expected, but God's wisdom led to a better outcome. How did God's will lead you in a direction you couldn't have foreseen?

Extended Reflection Prompts:

- How can you trust God's wisdom over your own understanding?
- What plans in your life are you surrendering to God today?
- How can you submit your decisions to God's counsel, knowing He leads to the best outcome?

Practical Application/Action Step:

Reflect on a plan or decision you are facing and submit it to God today. Trust that His wisdom will guide you and bring the best result.

Prayer:

Lord, I trust in Your wisdom and submit my plans to You. Help me to follow Your guidance in every area of my life. In Jesus' name, Amen.

Meditative Thought:

'No counsel can stand against the wisdom of the Lord, and I choose to trust it today.'

Wisdom Quote:

'No wisdom, no understanding, no counsel can stand against the Lord.' – Proverbs 21:30

Day 22: Proverbs 14:8 (NKJV) *Scripture:*

"The wisdom of the prudent is to understand his way, but the folly of fools is deceit." — Proverbs 14:8

Declaration:

I walk with spiritual prudence. I understand the path God has for me and reject the deceit of the enemy. In Jesus' name, Amen.

Biblical Context and Explanation:

This verse contrasts wisdom and folly. The prudent person understands the path they are on because they seek God's direction. Foolishness, on the other hand, leads to deceit and confusion, causing people to stumble. Wisdom involves discernment, and spiritual prudence helps us to navigate life's choices with clarity and integrity.

Character Study – The Prudence of Nehemiah:

Nehemiah demonstrated great prudence when he led the rebuilding of Jerusalem's walls. His wisdom in planning, prayer, and action helped him to understand the challenges ahead and avoid the distractions and deceit of his enemies (Nehemiah 2:17-20). Nehemiah's prudence in listening to God and moving forward in faith led to a successful outcome.

Real-Life Example:

Reflect on a time when you had to understand your path before making a decision. How did spiritual prudence guide you in that situation?

Extended Reflection Prompts:

- In what areas do you need to recognize your own limitations and rely on God's strength instead of your own?
- How can humility play a role in the process of spiritual prudence?
- What steps can you take today to reject deceit and walk with wisdom?

Practical Application/Action Step:

Spend time in prayer, asking God to help you understand your current path with clarity. Seek His guidance and wisdom in any areas where you may feel uncertain.

Prayer:

Lord, I ask for spiritual prudence to guide my decisions. Help me to recognize where I need Your strength and discernment. I reject the deceit of the enemy and choose to walk in Your wisdom. In Jesus' name, Amen.

Meditative Thought:

"Spiritual prudence helps me understand my path and reject the deceit of the enemy."

Wisdom Quote:

"Wisdom is the ability to see things as they really are, and prudence is the ability to act accordingly." – Anonymous

Day 23: Proverbs 15:2 (NKJV) *Scripture:*

"The tongue of the wise uses knowledge rightly, but the mouth of fools pours forth foolishness." — Proverbs 15:2

Declaration:

My tongue is filled with wisdom. I speak life, truth, and encouragement. The Holy Spirit gives me grace and power to build others up. In Jesus' name, Amen.

Biblical Context and Explanation:

This verse speaks about the power of words. The wise use their words to impart knowledge and encourage others, while foolish people speak without understanding, often causing harm. Wisdom in speech involves choosing words that build others up, bring clarity, and reflect God's truth.

Character Study – Jesus' Wisdom in His Words:

Jesus was a master of using words wisely. His words were filled with grace and truth, bringing healing, hope, and correction. In Matthew 12:34, He said, "Out of the abundance of the heart, the mouth speaks." Jesus' speech was always thoughtful, intentional, and wise, even when confronting challenging situations.

Real-Life Example:

Think of a time when your words encouraged or helped someone. How did you feel afterward, and how did it impact that person?

Extended Reflection Prompts:

- Wisdom often requires waiting on God's timing. Reflect on a situation in which you've had to wait for God's perfect timing. What did you learn during the waiting period? •
- How can you trust God
  more deeply in your current waiting season?
- What steps can you take today to ensure your words reflect wisdom and encouragement?

Practical Application/Action Step:

Pay attention to your words today. Seek to speak life, truth, and encouragement in your conversations, and be mindful of how your speech affects others.

Prayer:

Father, I ask for Your wisdom to guide my words. Help me to speak life and truth, building others up and encouraging them. May my tongue reflect Your grace and wisdom in all my conversations. In Jesus' name, Amen.

Meditative Thought:

"My words are powerful. I choose to speak wisdom and encouragement today."

Wisdom Quote:

"The words you speak can either build or tear down. Choose wisely." – Anonymous

Day 24: Proverbs 16:16 (NKJV) *Scripture:*

"How much better to get wisdom than gold! And to get understanding is to be chosen rather than silver." — Proverbs 16:16

Declaration:

I choose wisdom over wealth and understanding over status. I pursue the eternal treasures found in Christ. In Jesus' name, Amen.

Biblical Context and Explanation:

Proverbs 16:16 emphasizes the priceless value of wisdom and understanding. While wealth and status are temporary, wisdom provides lasting value. Wisdom leads to a fulfilling life and eternal rewards, far beyond what money or fame can offer.

Character Study – Solomon's Priorities:

When Solomon became king, God offered him anything he desired. Solomon chose wisdom over wealth, and God granted him both (1 Kings 3:5-14). His decision to prioritize wisdom set him apart as one of the wealthiest and most respected rulers in history. Solomon understood that wisdom was a treasure that far outweighed material wealth.

Real-Life Example:

Think about a decision you made that prioritized wisdom over worldly gain. How did that choice lead to a more meaningful outcome?

Extended Reflection Prompts:

- How does wisdom influence your decision-making when faced with the temptation of worldly wealth and status?
- Reflect on a time when you chose wisdom over immediate gain. What was the long-term benefit of that decision?

- In what areas of your life can you further prioritize wisdom over material pursuits?

Practical Application/Action Step:

Today, take time to reflect on one area of your life where you may be tempted to chase after wealth or status. Choose to make a decision based on wisdom instead. Whether in your finances, career, or relationships, seek God's direction first and value His eternal treasures over temporary gains.

Prayer:

Lord, I choose to prioritize Your wisdom over the fleeting things of

this world. Help me to recognize that true fulfillment and lasting peace come from Your understanding. Teach me to make decisions that

reflect Your values and eternal rewards, and may I find contentment in Your wisdom above all else. In Jesus' name, Amen.

Meditative Thought:

"Wisdom is the true treasure, and it leads to eternal peace and joy."

Wisdom Quote:

"True wisdom is the ability to see what is eternal beyond the temporary distractions of wealth and status." – Anonymous

Day 25: Proverbs 17:27 (NKJV) *Scripture:*

"He who has knowledge spares his words, and a man of understanding is of a calm spirit." — Proverbs 17:27

Declaration:

I am slow to speak and quick to understand. God's wisdom brings me peace and composure, and I rest in His Spirit. In Jesus' name, Amen.

Biblical Context and Explanation:

This verse highlights the wisdom in being slow to speak and quick to listen. A person of wisdom doesn't rush to speak but chooses words carefully, recognizing that understanding and calmness are far more valuable than hastiness. Wisdom and understanding bring peace to the heart, mind, and spirit.

Character Study – Job's Patience and Wisdom:

Job is a model of wisdom in the midst of suffering. Despite his intense trials, he remained patient and controlled in his speech. Job did not speak rashly but trusted in God's timing and wisdom (Job 2:10). His calm spirit in the face of adversity reflected his deep understanding of God's sovereignty.

Real-Life Example:

Reflect on a time when you faced a challenge and practiced patience. How did your calm response affect the situation and those around you?

Extended Reflection Prompts:

- When you encounter difficulty, where do you turn for wisdom?
- How can you turn to God and His Word for guidance in challenging situations, rather than relying on worldly wisdom?
- How can being slow to speak and quick to understand bring peace to your relationships?

Practical Application/Action Step:

In a conversation today, choose to listen more than you speak. Practice being calm and measured in your response, seeking to understand before reacting.

Prayer:

Father, help me to be slow to speak and quick to understand. May Your wisdom bring calmness and peace to my spirit. Guide me to respond with patience and humility in every situation. In Jesus' name, Amen.

Meditative Thought:

"A calm spirit and wise words are the fruit of God's understanding in me."

Wisdom Quote:

"Wisdom is not just knowing when to speak, but when to listen." – Anonymous

---

Day 26: Proverbs 18:4 (NKJV) *Scripture:*

"The words of a man's mouth are deep waters; the wellspring of wisdom is a flowing brook." — Proverbs 18:4

Declaration:

The words I speak are filled with divine wisdom. The Holy Spirit flows through me like a living stream, refreshing and inspiring others. In Jesus' name, Amen.

Biblical Context and Explanation:

This verse speaks of the power of words. Words that are full of wisdom are like deep waters—life-giving and refreshing. The wellspring of wisdom, when it flows from the heart, can inspire and refresh others, much like a flowing brook. Wisdom in speech brings life and direction, pointing others toward the truth of God.

Character Study – The Apostle Paul's Words:

Paul's letters in the New Testament are filled with wisdom, offering

encouragement, correction, and instruction. His words flowed from the deep well of God's wisdom, bringing life to the churches he ministered to. He was a powerful example of how words filled with divine

wisdom can inspire and build up the body of Christ.

Real-Life Example:

Think of a time when your words encouraged or inspired someone. How did you feel afterward, and how did the Holy Spirit use your speech to impact them?

Extended Reflection Prompts:

- How do you allow the Holy Spirit to flow through your words?
- How can your speech become a wellspring of life to those around you?
- In what situations can you speak words of wisdom and encouragement today?

Practical Application/Action Step:

Today, focus on using your words to refresh and encourage others. Speak life into a situation, and be mindful of how your words can build others up.

Prayer:

Holy Spirit, fill my words with Your wisdom. Help me to speak life and encouragement to those around me. May my words flow like a refreshing brook, bringing peace and truth. In Jesus' name, Amen.

Meditative Thought:

"My words, filled with wisdom, can refresh and inspire others."

Wisdom Quote:

"Words filled with wisdom are like water to a thirsty soul." – Anonymous

---

Day 27: Proverbs 19:8 (NKJV) *Scripture:*

"He who gets wisdom loves his own soul; he who keeps understanding will find good." — Proverbs 19:8

Declaration:

I love my soul by walking in wisdom. I treasure understanding and keep it close, finding good in every step through Christ. In Jesus' name, Amen.

Biblical Context and Explanation:

This verse highlights the profound relationship between wisdom and a fulfilled life. Wisdom is not just for the mind, but it brings goodness to our soul. The person who treasures wisdom will find satisfaction, peace, and purpose in life.

Character Study – The Life of Solomon:

Solomon's life is a testament to the benefits of wisdom. His request for wisdom over riches (1 Kings 3:11-12) brought him peace and

prosperity. By seeking wisdom, Solomon found good in his reign, ruling Israel with justice and wisdom.

Real-Life Example:

Think about a time when you made a decision based on wisdom. How did it bring goodness to your life or soul? Reflect on the blessings of choosing wisdom.

Extended Reflection Prompts:

- How has wisdom brought goodness to your life?
- What decisions have you made based on wisdom that brought you peace or success?
- How can you grow in wisdom and understanding in the areas you value most?

Practical Application/Action Step:

Take time today to reflect on your choices and ask God for wisdom in a specific area of your life. Trust that He will guide you to make decisions that bring goodness to your soul.

Prayer:

Lord, I thank You for the wisdom that brings goodness to my life. Help me to walk in wisdom today and every day, making decisions that honor You and bring peace to my soul. In Jesus' name, Amen.

Meditative Thought:

'Wisdom brings goodness to my soul, and I choose to seek it today.'

Wisdom Quote:

'He who gets wisdom loves his soul, for wisdom brings peace and understanding.' – Proverbs 19:8

Day 28: Proverbs 11:14 (NKJV) Scripture:

"Where there is no counsel, the people fall; But in the multitude of counselors there is safety." — Proverbs 11:14

Declaration:

I seek godly counsel and embrace the wisdom of many. In trusting the guidance of those who walk in the truth, I find safety, protection, and clarity. I will not lean on my own understanding but will surround myself with wise and trusted advisors. In Jesus' name, Amen.

Biblical Context and Explanation:

Proverbs 11:14 emphasizes the importance of wise counsel. Without guidance from others, people can fall into mistakes or dangerous situations. The verse highlights that having many counselors— especially those who are grounded in godly wisdom—provides safety.

It's a reminder that we are not meant to navigate life alone but should seek guidance from others to walk in the paths of righteousness.

This principle is not just about listening to others but surrounding ourselves with people who offer biblical wisdom and direction, creating a safety net for our decisions.

Character Study – King Solomon's Wisdom in Leadership: King Solomon, the author of many of the Proverbs, understood the importance of counsel. As a young king, Solomon sought wisdom from God (1 Kings 3:5-14). Despite being given unparalleled wisdom by God, he also surrounded himself with wise advisors to guide him in leading the nation of Israel. This highlights that even those with great wisdom recognize the need for others' perspectives and guidance.

Solomon's life exemplifies how seeking counsel from others— whether in times of peace or challenge—can lead to stability and success. His reign was prosperous because he listened to wise advice and made decisions based on divine counsel.

Real-Life Example:

Think of a time when seeking counsel from trusted mentors or friends helped you avoid a difficult situation. Perhaps you were facing a career decision, a personal conflict, or a financial choice. How did their advice give you a clearer path and help you make a better decision?

In contrast, consider a situation where you didn't seek guidance and faced challenges as a result. What did you learn from that experience about the value of counsel?

Extended Reflection Prompts:

- How often do you seek counsel before making important decisions?
- Reflect on a time when wise counsel led you to safety or success. How did it impact your life?
- Do you surround yourself with a diverse group of trusted advisors? If not, how can you begin to build a stronger support network for future decisions?

- In what areas of your life do you feel you need more guidance? How can you actively seek counsel in those areas?

Practical Application/Action Step:

Take a moment today to identify a decision or situation where you could benefit from seeking counsel. Reach out to a trusted advisor—a mentor, pastor, or wise friend—and seek their input. Commit to being open to their guidance and prayerfully consider their wisdom. Implement what you learn in your decision-making process.

Prayer:

Lord, I thank You for the gift of wise counsel. I acknowledge that I am not meant to walk this journey alone. Help me to surround myself with wise and godly advisors who will lead me closer to Your will. May I listen with humility and trust that Your direction comes through others. Lead me safely along the path You have prepared for me. In Jesus' name, Amen.

Meditative Thought:

"In the multitude of counselors, I find safety. God's wisdom flows through others, guiding my steps."

Wisdom Quote:

"Plans are established by counsel, and by wise counsel, they succeed."

— Proverbs 15:22

Day 29: Proverbs 12:1 (NKJV)

Scripture:

"Whoever loves instruction loves knowledge, but he who hates correction is stupid." — Proverbs 12:1

Declaration:

I love instruction and seeking knowledge. I welcome correction and growth, trusting that God's wisdom will guide me toward His best plan. In Jesus' name, Amen.

Biblical Context and Explanation:

Proverbs 12:1 highlights the importance of embracing instruction and correction. Wisdom begins with a teachable heart, one that is open to learning and growing. Those who resist correction or avoid instruction close themselves off to growth and understanding. This verse encourages us to value guidance and wisdom, whether it comes from God's Word or through others. It's through correction and teaching that we are refined and led on the right path.

Character Study – The Teachable Spirit of King David:

King David was a man after God's own heart (Acts 13:22), and his willingness to receive correction played a key role in his spiritual growth. In 2 Samuel 12, when confronted by the prophet Nathan about his sin with Bathsheba, David repented with humility and sorrow. He didn't resist correction but accepted it, demonstrating a teachable spirit. God honored his humility and restored him. David's example teaches us that when we embrace correction and instruction, we grow in wisdom and understanding.

Real-Life Example:

Think about a time when you resisted correction or instruction. What was the result? Now, reflect on a time when you welcomed correction, and how did that decision lead to growth or success? How can you cultivate a teachable spirit moving forward?

Extended Reflection Prompts:

- How do you respond to correction or constructive feedback in your life?
- In what areas of your life do you need to be more open to instruction?
- How can you foster a humble and teachable heart in all aspects of life?
- What steps can you take today to learn from someone else's wisdom or experience?

Practical Application/Action Step:
Today, seek instruction in an area where you need growth. Whether through reading, mentorship, or feedback from others, choose to

embrace wisdom and correction. Reflect on the benefits of being open to learning and growing.

Prayer:

Lord, I love instruction and seek Your wisdom in all areas of my life. Help me to be humble and teachable, receiving corrections with a heart that desires to grow. Guide me to understand Your truth and apply it in every decision I make. In Jesus' name, Amen.

Meditative Thought:

"A teachable heart leads to wisdom, and wisdom leads to life."

Wisdom Quote:

"A wise person values correction, for it leads to growth and understanding." — Proverbs 12:1

Day 30: Proverbs 23:23 (NKJV) *Scripture:*

"Buy the truth, and do not sell it, also wisdom and instruction and understanding." — Proverbs 23:23

Declaration:

I hold fast to truth, wisdom, instruction, and understanding. I will not trade these treasures for anything temporary. In Jesus' name, Amen.

Biblical Context and Explanation:

Wisdom, truth, and understanding are invaluable treasures that should be cherished and upheld. Proverbs warns against giving up these gifts for fleeting gains. The truth and wisdom that come from God are priceless, and we are to protect and hold on to them.

Character Study – The Integrity of Job:

Job's life exemplified the importance of holding onto truth and wisdom even in the midst of loss and hardship. Despite his suffering, Job never gave up his faith or integrity. His steadfastness in truth brought restoration and blessings (Job 42:10).

Real Life Example:

Reflect on a time when you held onto wisdom or truth, even when faced with opposition. How did It strengthen you, and what did you learn from it?

Extended Reflection Prompts:

• How can you hold onto wisdom and truth in your current circumstances?
• What does it look like to prioritize truth over temporary gain?
• How can you avoid trading the wisdom of God for worldly pursuits?

Practical Application/Action Step:

Today, choose to hold fast to wisdom and truth in a specific situation. Trust that God's way leads to peace and lasting success.

Prayer:

Lord, I commit to holding fast to Your truth and wisdom. May I not trade Your understanding for anything temporary. Lead me today in Your path of righteousness. In Jesus' name, Amen.

Meditative Thought:

'I will buy the truth and never sell it, for it is my guiding light.'

Wisdom Quote:

'Wisdom is more valuable than gold, and truth is worth more than riches.' – Proverbs 23:23

Day 31: Proverbs 24:14 (NKJV) *Scripture:*

"So shall the knowledge of wisdom be to your soul; if you have found it, there is a prospect, and your hope will not be cut off." — Proverbs 24:14

Declaration:

The wisdom of God nourishes my soul. My future is secure, my hope is alive, and my destiny is fulfilled in Christ. In Jesus' name, Amen.

Biblical Context and Explanation:

The knowledge of wisdom is not only a guide for the present but also brings hope and a secure future. Wisdom nourishes our soul, enabling us to walk confidently in the promises of God.

Character Study – The Fulfillment of God's Promise:

The wisdom we receive from God helps us to fulfill His promises. Wisdom is a life-sustaining force, directing us to God's destiny for our lives. It secures our future and ensures that we walk in God's plans.

Real Life Example:

Think about a time when God's wisdom brought clarity and hope to your future. How did it shape your decisions and provide direction?

Extended Reflection Prompts:

- How has wisdom impacted your view of the future?
- In what ways has God's wisdom brought hope and security to your life?
- How can you cultivate wisdom to continue walking in God's will?

Practical Application/Action Step:

Reflect on your future today. Ask God to continue guiding you in wisdom and to give you peace and hope for what's ahead.

Prayer:

Father, I thank You for the wisdom that secures my future. Help me to walk in Your plans, knowing that my destiny is in Your hands. Guide me today with Your wisdom and bring peace to my soul. In Jesus 'name, Amen.

Meditative Thought:

'God's wisdom secures my future, and I trust His plan for my life.'

Wisdom Quote:

'Wisdom nourishes the soul and gives hope for the future.' – Proverbs 24:14

Journaling Prompts

Take a moment to reflect on the wisdom you've encountered over the past 31 days. These prompts are designed to help you internalize the truth of God's Word and how it has impacted your life.

- How has your understanding of wisdom changed over the course of these 31 days?
- Reflect on a declaration that stood out to you the most. How did it impact your thoughts, actions, or relationships?
- What steps will you take in the future to continue walking in God's wisdom?
- In what areas of your life do you feel you need to apply wisdom more intentionally?

- What new insights have you gained about trusting God with your decisions?

Closing Prayer

Father, we thank You for the wisdom You've poured into us during these 31 days. May we continue to walk in Your light, guided by the Holy Spirit. We declare that the wisdom we've gained will bear fruit in every area of our lives. May we be a light to others, reflecting Your truth and love. We trust in Your plan and know that Your wisdom will lead us to our destiny. In Jesus' name, Amen.

About the Author

Risa Stegall is passionate about guiding others to walk in God's wisdom and truth. With a heart rooted in faith and a voice led by the Holy Spirit, she equips individuals to align their lives with God's purpose through practical, Spirit-filled teachings.

As the author of *Walking in Wisdom: 31 Declarations That Change Everything*, *Walking in Godliness: A Daily Journey Through Proverbs to Reflect God's Character*, and *The Choice That Changed Everything*, Risa empowers readers to grow in clarity, spiritual discernment, and intentional living.

Her mission is to help others experience the transformative power of God's wisdom in everyday decisions—bringing peace, direction, and lasting change to their lives.

To connect or explore more resources:
Email: shepherdsword@shepherdswordpublishing.com
Website: shepherdswordpublishing.com

.

www.ingramcontent.com/pod-product-compliance
Lightning Source LLC
Chambersburg PA
CBHW051433090426
42737CB00014B/2953